King Arthur

BY
Mike Ashley

This edition first published by
Parragon Book Service Ltd in 1996

Parragon Book Service Ltd
Unit 13–17 Avonbridge Trading Estate
Atlantic Road, Avonmouth
Bristol BS11 9QD

Produced by Magpie Books,
an imprint of Robinson Publishing

ISBN 0 75251 596 9

A copy of the British Library Cataloguing in Publication
Data is available from the British Library.

Typeset by Whitelaw & Palmer Ltd, Glasgow
Printed in Singapore

KING ARTHUR

The image of the chivalrous, courtly Arthur, defending Britain against all threats and enemies, has long been a proud part of our heritage. For the most part, that legend is total fabrication, yet tucked away are hints of the truth, folk memories of the days when the real Arthur, the only man capable of uniting the native British, stood fast against the invading Saxons, and for forty years managed to keep alive the last golden glow of the ancient world.

Most of our images of Arthur rely on stories we heard or read as children, perhaps from the books by Howard Pyle, Rosemary Sutcliffe or Roger Lancelyn Green, or on the Walt Disney film *The Sword in the Stone*, based on the book by T. H. White. All of these draw upon the stories in *Le Morte d'Arthur*, a compendium of Arthurian tales pulled together by Thomas Malory in the fifteenth century. Although the exploits of Arthur were first recorded by Geoffrey of Monmouth in his *History of the Kings of Britain*, it is Malory's work that remains the fundamental source of the Arthurian legend as we know it. But how much is fact and how much is fiction?

To discover the facts about the real Arthur we need to consider not only the times in which he lived, but also the times in which his legend was born, and that way we can try and piece together both lives of King Arthur. First, the legend.

ARTHUR'S BIRTH

There is no single life of Arthur. Because of their many sources, the Arthurian legends often contradict each other, which is part of their mystery and fascination. And by the time of Malory, many of the heroic episodes initially associated with Arthur had moved to his knights, and Arthur had become a rather tragic figure.

The legend begins with Uther Pendragon, the new overlord of Britain. He is at war against

Merlin with his mother

Gorlois, the Duke of Cornwall. Uther summons Gorlois and his wife, Ygraine, to his court and upon seeing Ygraine, Uther falls in love with her. Gorlois hides Ygraine in his castle at Tintagel, but Uther arranges for Merlin to cast a glamour over Ygraine so that she perceives Uther in the form of Gorlois. Uther seduces Ygraine and Arthur is conceived.

Before working Uther's deceit, Merlin agreed with the king that the child of that union would be given to Merlin to raise. Merlin takes the young Arthur and gives him to Sir Ector to foster; and so Arthur and Ector's son Kay are raised as brothers. During this period Merlin would have taught Arthur much of the wisdom of the ancients, but little is said of this in the chronicles.

Arthur was unaware of his true parentage or

of his half-sisters. Ygraine and Gorlois had three daughters: Morgause, also called Anna, who later married King Lot of Orkney and became the mother of Gawain, Gareth, Gaheris and Agravaine; Morgan, later called Morgan Le Fay, who married King Urien of Rheged and was the mother of Owain; and Elaine, who married King Nentres of Garlot.

Gorlois dies soon after Arthur's birth and Uther marries Ygraine. A few years later Uther falls ill and King Lot becomes overlord of Britain. He usurps Uther's power and war breaks out. The conflict is unresolved by the death of Uther, some say of poison.

ARTHUR THE KING

Merlin requests the Archbishop to summon all
the vassal kings to London on Christmas Day
where the Lord will perform a miracle in the
choosing of a new king. The kings assemble.
To their surprise they see, in the churchyard of
the cathedral, a stone, on top of which is a
sword embedded in an anvil. Written on the
anvil are the words: WHOSO PULLETH OUT
THIS SWORD OF THIS STONE AND ANVIL IS
RIGHTWISE KING BORN OF ALL ENGLAND.

Try as they might none of the kings can remove the sword. For over a week the Archbishop awaits a sign. On New Year's Day, Sir Ector arrives with Kay and Arthur to join in the jousting. Kay has lost his sword and Arthur, unaware of the significance, pulls the sword from the anvil, and gives it to Kay. Sir Ector realizes what had happened and asks Arthur to show him again. All of the kings gather around as Merlin replaces the sword. Again they try, but only Arthur can remove it. Although he is little more than 15 years old, Arthur is recognized as king.

Preparations are made for Arthur's coronation at his court at Caerleon. Despite the miracle of the sword in the stone, some kings, urged on by King Lot, doubt Arthur's right to the throne. They question Merlin who reveals Arthur's parentage. Though some accept this, others rebel and within the first months of his reign Arthur finds himself facing an uprising.

Arthur forms an alliance with King Bors of Gaul and King Ban of Benwick (or Bayonne) in France. To gain their support, Arthur has to help them in battle against their enemy, King Claudas. (Claudas was probably synonymous with Clovis, the king of the Franks from AD 481–511 and thus a contemporary of the real Arthur.) Ban and Bors accompany Arthur back to Britain where he raises a force and goes into battle against the unfaithful kings. The battle is long and hard and many thousands die, but still it is undecided. In the midst of the battle, Arthur hears that his friend, King Leodegrance of Cameliard, is being harried by King Rience of North Wales. Rience has a cloak made of the beards of defeated kings and he sends a message to Arthur that he will

Arthur's coronation

complete the cloak with Arthur's beard. Arthur, Ban and Bors ride against King Rience and, in a fierce battle which leaves thousands more dead, defeat him.

Whilst Arthur is fighting Rience the rebel kings learn of a further invasion by the Saxons who are destroying the land. The kings realize that whilst they fight Arthur, they are leaving their lands in danger and promptly state their allegiance to Arthur and return to defend their kingdoms.

Arthur, supported by his kings and their knights, leads the British against the Saxons, fighting battles that spread across the north of England. At length, in Caledon Wood, Arthur's men surround the Saxons and lay siege, starving them out. The Saxons are despatched from Britain, but they return to a more southerly point and again begin to lay waste. Arthur, supported by the Church of Rome, marches on them and soundly defeats them at Badon.

With Arthur battling the Saxons, the Scottish and Irish Celts believe they can conquer the north, but the Saxons defeated, Arthur marches on the Scots and Irish. The fighting is so violent that their bishops beg for mercy. Within an unspecified but relatively short period, Arthur has restored peace to the land, a peace that would last for 40 years. He is probably about 20 years old.

THE SEEDS OF DESTRUCTION

Of his vassal kings, only Lot remains subversive. He sends his wife, Morgause, accompanied by her sons, to spy out the court. Morgause is unknown to Arthur and does not betray her origins, so he is unaware that she is his half-sister. He seduces her, and she conceives Mordred, who is thereby both Arthur's son and nephew. Thus are sown the seeds of Arthur's destruction. Interestingly, both Arthur and Mordred are conceived in deception.

At about this time Arthur has a vision about the wasting of the Land that disturbs him. To recover from the dream he goes on a hunt and, at a pool, sees a bizarre animal. It has the body of a leopard, the hindquarters of a lion, the feet of a deer, and the head of a snake. From its stomach comes the sound of hounds baying. Because of this the creature is called the Questing Beast. It is the offspring of a girl who slept with the Devil. At this same time Arthur learns from Merlin that he has slept with his half-sister, and the significance of this and the Questing Beast worry Arthur.

Merlin adds to his disquiet by prophesying that a child born that Mayday will be Arthur's ruin, and that all children born that day should be killed. Arthur cannot bring himself to kill these infants, but he declares that all children of noble birth, born in the last two months should be sent to him. He then casts all the infants adrift in a ship. The ship founders on rocks, and many of the infants perish, but amongst those saved is Mordred.

Guinevere, William Morris

ARTHUR'S COURT

Settled at last in his kingdom, Arthur looks for a wife. He has long admired Guinevere, daughter of his close ally Leodegrance (or Cador), Duke of Cameliard. Guinevere was believed to be descended from Roman stock, and was considered the most beautiful lady in the land.

As part of the marriage arrangement, Arthur acquires the Round Table, made by Merlin for King Uther, which Leodegrance had inherited. It is at this table that Arthur commands his most noble knights to sit. To earn that right the knights must undertake deeds of considerable valour and heroism. Only one seat at the table remains empty, called the Siege Perilous by Merlin, and this can only be occupied by the most holy and perfect of knights. This means that once the Round Table is filled it is complete in both a physical and spiritual sense. But any who are unworthy and try to take the seat would die.

The need for knights to prove their worth is a significant part of the Arthurian legend. Young men from all over Britain flocked to Arthur's court in the hope of becoming a knight and being honoured with a seat at the Round Table. Although in legend the Round Table is regarded as a physical object at which Arthur held counsel, it was equally the name

The Round Table

given by Arthur to his highest order of most noble knights. These most noble knights would have been Arthur's closest advisers and were the equivalent of his court or parliament.

Not all of Arthur's knights were Knights of the Round Table, and the number accorded this honour ranges from twelve to over a thousand. The smaller figure is the more likely and although the names vary, the core of these knights included, at various stages, Kay, Ector, Erec, Bors, Bedivere, Yvain, Gawain, Gaheris, Perceval, Pelleas, Tristan, Lancelot and lastly Galahad.

We need not assume that Arthur had one single capital. It is likely he had residences all over Britain, especially considering the many sites associated with him. The name of Camelot, the many towered castle of the

French romancers, was first mentioned by Chrétien de Troyes. Prior to this, Geoffrey of Monmouth had located Arthur's capital at Caerleon in South Wales, based on an earlier description as City of the Legions, an old Roman title. This, though, would apply equally, and probably better, to either Chester or Carlisle. Others have argued that Colchester, Britain's oldest city, which the Romans called Camulodunum, was the location of Camelot, whilst the site of Cadbury Castle in Somerset also has much support.

In the early days of his reign, Arthur travelled throughout his kingdom, often in the company of Merlin who disguised Arthur so that he would not be recognized. On one journey Arthur is challenged by King Pellinore of Northumberland. The two fight. Pellinore casts Arthur to the ground and is ready to strike the fatal blow when he is struck by one of Merlin's spells. When Pellinore recovers and learns of Arthur's identity he submits to the king.

In the fight Arthur's sword has broken. Merlin takes him to a nearby lake. There, in a chapel, he meets the Lady of the Lake who shows Arthur a sword held in a hand rising from the middle of the lake. Arthur takes a boat out and claims the sword for his own. Merlin asks Arthur which he feels is more precious, the sword or its scabbard. Arthur, looking at the beautiful sword, long and straight with its hilt encrusted in jewels, replies without hesitation that the sword is the more pleasing. But Merlin counsels that he is unwise, for all the time he keeps the scabbard beside him he will remain unharmed, but without the scabbard he will one day be defeated. Here was a lesson that the king was no king without the support of his people.

MORGAN LE FAY

Arthur entrusts Excalibur to his half-sister, Morgan le Fay, unaware that she is plotting against him, seeking ways to weaken his power. One day Arthur is out hunting with King Urien and Sir Accolon of Gaul. They chase a deer for so long that they are exhausted and look for lodgings for the night. Arthur sees a stretch of water on which is a ship bedecked in silk. Unbeknown to them, the three are bewitched by Morgan le Fay and, as night falls, she lures them onto the boat. When they wake the next morning, Urien finds he is back in Camelot, Accolon is on a perilous hillside and Arthur is imprisoned in the castle of Sir Damas, a vile knight who challenges all comers to fight his brother Sir Ontzlake, with whom he has a dispute. Arthur agrees to fight Ontzlake provided all the prisoners in the castle are freed.

In the meantime, Accolon meets a dwarf, an envoy of Morgan le Fay, who brings Accolon Excalibur in its scabbard, and tells the knight that he must help Sir Ontzlake the next day. Accolon finds Ontzlake recovering from a wound and agrees that he will undertake the knight's next challenge. By this deception, Morgan pits Sir Accolon armed with Excalibur against King Arthur, to whom she has handed a fake Excalibur.

The battle between Sir Accolon and Arthur is

Morgan le Fay

hard and long. Because he wields Excalibur, Accolon nearly defeats Arthur, but the Lady of the Lake, seeing the battle, sends an enchantment which causes Excalibur to fall from Accolon's hand into Arthur's. It is only as Arthur strikes the death-blow that he realizes who his opponent was. He tries to save Accolon, but so deep are the wounds that Accolon dies four days later.

Morgan is furious that Arthur lives. She finds him sleeping in the abbey where Accolon has died. As he sleeps she tries to steal Excalibur, but is unable to take it without waking him. However, she does ease the scabbard free and flees with that. When Arthur wakes he learns of his sister's visit and hurries in pursuit, but Morgan has disguised herself and Arthur is unable to find her or the scabbard.

Morgan continues to plot against Arthur. Anonymously, she sends him a gift of a precious cloak steeped in poison. The Lady of the Lake warns Arthur against wearing it without first commanding that she who sent it should wear it. Arthur takes this to mean the young girl who has delivered the cloak, and he commands her to wear it. No sooner does she don it than the acid burns her to death. Arthur now realizes the full treachery of his sister and thereafter the two remain mortal enemies.

Morgan does achieve one triumph. Although the Lady of the Lake supports Arthur she despises Merlin. The Lady of the Lake has been entrusted with the infant son of Ban of Benwick, Lancelot, and when Lancelot has grown to manhood she delivers him to Arthur's court. She goes disguised as the enchantress Nimuë whom Merlin had not seen before and the old mage falls under her spell. She lures him away from Arthur's court and imprisons him under a stone, where he remains to this day. Arthur is now without his chief adviser who has steered his course since his birth. On that day, Arthur's star begins to fall.

Merlin and Nimuë

THE YEARS OF PERIL

According to some histories Arthur continued to expand his kingdom. Having subdued Britain, and protected her against the Saxon invaders, he sought to conquer and defeat Ireland, France, Germany, Norway, and so on throughout western Europe, establishing an Arthurian empire to rival the Romans.

Others, though, recognize that Arthur became cautious about leaving his court. Although many adventures are still ascribed to him, we find that as he reached his middle years he tended to hold court at Camelot rather than venture forth. Many would come to Camelot seeking advice and help, and invariably Arthur would despatch a knight to help any damsel in distress, but he seldom went himself. We even find, in the case of Lynette, who came seeking help for her sister against the evil Red Knight, Arthur rebuking her for wasting their time. The loss of the scabbard was beginning to have its insidious effect. We see here a kingdom which, after several years of peace, has become decadent. It is during these days that Lancelot becomes captivated by Guinevere's beauty and falls in love with her.

A key event in this love triangle comes with the abduction of Guinevere by Sir Meleagaunce. Meleagaunce was the son of

Lancelot rescuing Guinevere

King Bagdemagus of Gorre, a small kingdom either in Cumbria or the Isle of Man. Bagdemagus was annoyed when he was over-looked by Arthur who raised Sir Tor to the Round Table in his stead. Meleagaunce, seeking to avenge his father, abducts Guinevere with every intention of raping her. It is not Arthur who sets out to recover her but Lancelot. It is a perilous journey for Lancelot – one of the most exciting in all of the romances, involving Lancelot passing through the portals of death itself – but at length he is victorious. The rescue brings the two closer together – of which Arthur cannot be unaware although he seems to turn a blind eye to the situation.

At first only Lord Galehaut of the Faraway Isles knows of Lancelot's love for Guinevere, and it is he who arranges for them to meet one night. News spreads of their liaison. One day Lancelot arrives at Corbenic where King Pelles hopes that Lancelot will wed his daughter Elaine. He contrives for the two to meet, claiming that Guinevere is staying at his castle, and then slips a drug into Lancelot's wine so that he believes Elaine is Guinevere. The child of their union is Galahad, the purest knight of all.

Arthur had his own amorous adventures. In one legend he is lured into the Forest Perilous by the sorceress Annowre who wants him as her lover. She slips a ring of forgetfulness over his finger so that he forgets Guinevere. However, the Lady of the Lake learns of the circumstances and, before any dishonour can occur, Arthur is rescued by Sir Tristan. One legend has it that Guinevere has a twin sister whom she substitutes in her place while she dallies with Lancelot, and Arthur none the wiser. Here we see an Arthur who may have been a heroic warrior but was not a passionate lover.

It is interesting that though children are ascribed to Arthur, none of them, apart from the incestuous Mordred, made any significant claim to fame. Few of Arthur's sons seem to be children of Guinevere; they were old enough to have grown into manhood by the early part of Arthur's reign, suggesting they were illegitimate children of earlier liaisons. Indeed one, called Arthuret, was the child of rape. Another, Loholt, did become a Knight of the Round Table, but was subsequently killed in anger by Sir Kay; whilst Amr was killed by Arthur himself in a fit of anger.

These incidents do not show a king in full

control of either his kingdom or his emotions and add to the feeling that in later years Arthur's kingdom was falling into decline. This gives King Lot an opportunity to try and regain the kingdom. The uprising is brief, and it is not Arthur but King Pellinore, who kills King Lot. Pellinore pursues Lot's army into the north of Scotland, devastating the land en route, but he encounters Lot's son, Gawain, who kills him.

The peace and tranquillity of the kingdom is now severely under threat. Britain is ravaged by plague and pestilence. Historically, there was a plague that swept through Europe in the middle of the sixth century killing, it is said, one person in three. This epidemic was remembered in folk-memory as being caused by the Dolorous Stroke prophecied by Merlin and inflicted by Sir Balin upon Sir Pellam.

Lancelot and Guinevere

Balin was one of Arthur's most heroic knights, though he had a tendency to slaughter anyone on sight. At one stage he incurred the anger of King Arthur by killing the Lady of the Lake (more probably one of her maidens) but he redeemed himself by capturing King Rience, who continued to annoy Arthur with his taunts. On one of his quests Balin encountered an invisible knight, Sir Garlon, whom he succeeded in killing. Balin was challenged by Garlon's brother, Sir Pellam, which led to the most arduous combat Balin ever fought. During the fight Balin's sword was broken, and he fled through Sir Pellam's castle until he found a lance. He was not aware that this was the Holy Lance of Longinus, the very lance which had pierced Jesus's side on the cross. Balin grabbed the Lance and turned in time for Sir Pellam to run onto the point. With the death of Sir Pellam the Dolorous Stroke was

struck, and famine and pestilence fell over the kingdom. Sir Balin wandered through the waste land, and encountered his brother, Sir Balan, whom he did not recognize. Balan was the guardian of a castle, challenging all comers. The two fought and killed each other.

As the Land darkens Arthur looks for a sign. At the Feast of Pentecost at Camelot, Arthur and his knights have a vision of the Holy Grail. The Grail was one of the dishes from which Jesus had fed at the Last Supper, though in later years the word has come to mean the chalice from which he drank and which was believed to have held the blood of Christ as it dropped from his body on the Cross. As the Lance of Longinus had destroyed the Land, so the Blood of Christ could restore it. This Christian belief, a later addition to the legends, bears some comparison with the legendary Horn or Cauldron of Plenty – a vessel which never empties no matter how much you drink from it. The Grail had been brought to Britain by Joseph of Arimathea and was now guarded in the Grail Castle by the Fisher King. It was believed only the most pure knight would gain the Grail and only then if he asked the right question.

In the later legends it is Arthur's knights who set out on the Quest, in particular Gawain, Perceval, Lancelot, Bors and Galahad; different legends have different knights completing the quest. In earlier legends it is Arthur who seeks the Grail, as one would expect of an heroic king. Arthur travels with his knights into Ireland and from there into the world of faëry in order to bargain with the King of the Faëries and gain the Horn of Plenty. The quest is a near disaster with only seven men returning

Galahad preparing for knighthood

alive from the mysterious world of Annwn.

Whilst Arthur's Quest for the Horn of Plenty is a rousing heroic tale, the Quests by the various knights are more spiritual, their adventures and sacrifices closely allied to the twelfth- and thirteenth-century Crusades. Despite the eventual success of the Quest, and the return of life to the Land, peace is not restored to the kingdom. If anything the rivalry becomes more intense. At a feast held in London, Sir Patrise, is poisoned by an apple. His cousin, Sir Mador, accuses the Queen of murder. The King is amazed to find that none of the knights present will support Guinevere and fight on her behalf. At length Sir Lancelot learns of the situation and champions the Queen against Sir Mador.

In these latter days of Arthur's kingdom, what

remains of the Roman Empire becomes envious of his power. The Emperor, Lucius, sends a letter to Arthur ordering that he submit and pay tribute. Arthur refuses and gathers together an army of over 180,000 to march on Rome. There is little doubt that Arthur would have conquered Rome, for he defeated all opposition en route, but as he camps at the very outskirts of the city, news comes to him of treachery in his kingdom.

Arthur had left Guinevere in authority, supported by Mordred. However, Mordred had seized the throne and seduced the Queen, and moreover, he had brought an army of Saxons into Britain, with promise of land if they supported him. Arthur gives up his campaign on Rome and returns in haste to Britain. He first meets Mordred in Kent, at Richborough, near Sandwich, where

Mordred is defeated. But the traitor escapes and retrenches at Winchester. Guinevere, learning that Arthur has returned, flees to a nunnery.

Later legends have a different reason for Arthur's absence from Britain. In these tales, Arthur learns from Mordred of Guinevere's adultery with Lancelot. Once the news becomes common knowledge, Arthur is bound to seek honour, even against the bravest and most famous of his knights. Initially he orders Sir Mordred and Sir Agravaine to seize Lancelot, but Lancelot kills Agravaine and escapes. Arthur prepares to burn Guinevere at the stake for her adultery but Lancelot rescues her, killing many of the bravest knights in the process, and takes her to his castle at Joyous Gard. Arthur lays siege. The Companionship of the Round Table is now split between the supporters of Arthur and those of Lancelot, but in the ensuing battle when an opportunity presents itself to strike Arthur, Lancelot refrains.

Such is the threat to the world that even the Pope writes to Arthur from Rome seeking an end to the plight. At length Lancelot delivers Guinevere to Arthur and, with a retinue of knights, exiles himself from the kingdom. Arthur, still determined to defeat Lancelot, sets off in pursuit along with Sir Gawain, whose brothers Lancelot has killed. It is during this absence that Mordred seizes the kingdom, claiming that Arthur has been killed in his battle with Lancelot and that he is the rightful heir. Arthur returns and meets Mordred at Dover. In the battle Gawain is killed.

Arthur fighting Mordred

ARTHUR'S FINAL DAYS

So it is that Arthur and his remaining knights come to fight Mordred and his army at Camlann. The exact location of Camlann remains in dispute. Tradition places it in Cornwall, near the River Camel at Slaughterbridge, but there are also claims that it was near Dolgellau in Wales, or at Camboglanna, near Birdoswald along Hadrian's Wall.

The battle is one of wholesale slaughter and at

the end Mordred is killed and Arthur mortally wounded. Only Sir Lucan and Sir Bedivere (or in earlier tales Sir Griflet) survive. Arthur instructs Bedivere to return Excalibur to the Lady of the Lake. The knight finds it difficult to cast such a beautiful sword into the Lake and twice hides it in the bushes instead. Arthur knows he lies, and the third time Bedivere throws the sword far into the Lake. A hand rises from the water, catches the sword by the hilt, brandishes it three times and withdraws into the lake. When he tells Arthur this, the King knows that the knight has performed his task, and prepares to die.

Arthur commands Bedivere and Lucan to carry him to the lake. Lucan is so sorely wounded that he dies from the effort. A boat bearing Morgan and her maidens arrives and carries Arthur's body away to the Isle of

Bedivere casts Excalibur into the Lake

Avalon, there to heal. Britain is to await his return in times of peril.

The Golden Age of Britain has passed, with most of her famous knights dead. Lancelot, hearing of Mordred's treachery, hurries to Britain to aid Arthur, but is too late. He finds Guinevere in a nunnery, but she soon dies, and not long afterward Lancelot pines away in his castle. Sir Bedivere, wandering the land after the battle, comes to a hermitage, where, he learns, Morgan had brought the body of Arthur who has since died. Bedivere remains in the hermitage and dies soon after.

Arthur is succeeded as king by his brother-in-law Constantine, Duke of Cornwall, who continues to do battle against the supporters of Mordred, at length defeating them. (Constantine was one of the kings rebuked by the sixth-century writer Gildas in *De Excidio Britanniae* as an evil and immoral king.) It seems the perils of Arthur's reign live on after him, and it is not many years before the Saxons overrun the land and Arthur's kingdom has gone for ever.

Arthur's final earthly resting place is not known, though many have conjectured. Whether it is Glastonbury, where the monks at the abbey claimed they had found the bones of Arthur and Guinevere in 1191, or the Isle of Man, which was also the believed site of the Grail Castle, or Bardsey Island off the coast of Wales, or Iona or even the Scilly Isles perhaps matters little. Arthur's true resting place is in our hearts. He has lived in the memory of man for over fifty generations, recalling a hero who defended the island against every conceivable foe, only to be

Arthur lying in Avalon

defeated by treachery within his own house.

The story of Arthur's life is so complex that it is unlikely to have been the creation of just one man, so where did Malory obtain his ideas, and where did the legend of Arthur come from?

THE BIRTH OF
THE LEGEND

The Arthur of legend began to emerge in the
writings of the Welsh sometime after the end
of the seventh century. Although no written
texts survive earlier than the twelfth century, it
is likely that stories were set down in writing
at least two centuries earlier, probably during
the reign of Hywel Dda who ruled a more-or-
less united Wales in the middle of the tenth
century. The oldest surviving story about
Arthur is 'Kilhwch and Olwen'. This is a

rousing adventure tale about a young man called Kilhwch who is cursed by his step-mother and falls in love with Olwen, the daughter of a giant. Kilhwch goes to the court of King Arthur, his cousin, for help, and Arthur sends seven of his most valorous knights to help Kilhwch in his quest. They find Olwen but her father, the giant Ysbaddaden, forbids her to marry Kilhwch unless he and his friends can accomplish a series of impossible tasks. They return to Arthur who leads the warriors in their quest to achieve these tasks.

Arthur is portrayed as a mighty king capable of supernatural feats. He was without doubt the national hero of the Welsh, who yearned for his return. His significance became even greater when the Welsh, having established a peaceful alliance with the Saxons, came under threat from the Vikings and Normans throughout the tenth and eleventh centuries. The Welsh long believed that there would come a time when they would rise up and defeat the invaders and the kingdom of Arthur would be restored. The Norman conquerors of Britain needed to quell that belief, and the simplest way was to make Arthur their own hero, to recognize his triumphs and victories. The Norman kings would have been well aware of the Arthurian legend, not just in Britain, but in their neighbouring province of Brittany, in France. Brittany had been settled by Celts escaping from the Saxon invasion in the fifth century, before the emergence of Arthur, but refugees from Britain settled there later, bringing with them the tales of Arthur.

In the early years of the twelfth century the Normans were in constant battle against the Welsh who were regaining their strength.

There was every possibility that the Welsh might overrun the Normans and regain Britain. It was against this background that Geoffrey of Monmouth wrote his *Historia Regum Britanniae* (*History of the Kings of Britain*), which was dedicated to Robert, Earl of Gloucester, the illegitimate son of Henry I. It is possible that Robert, whose lands were under constant threat from the Welsh, directly commissioned the work. There was some agitation over Geoffrey's delay in completing the book, which had been started around the year 1130. Geoffrey states that he was translating into Latin a book originally written in Welsh. That book has never been found, though that is no reason to doubt its existence, but it is possible that as he was translating he was urged by others in power to incorporate as much as possible about the Welsh heroes of old, including Arthur. Geoffrey was himself of either Welsh or Breton descent, and because he styled himself as Gaufridus Monemutensis (Geoffrey of Monmouth) we must assume that he was either born or raised in that town. His connections and affiliations to Wales were therefore probably sincere, and he would have enjoyed embellishing the legends of old and converting them into history.

Geoffrey's book sets Arthur centre stage and shows how, almost single handedly, he fought off all invaders, established a Golden Age of peace and conquered most of Europe. The treachery of Mordred led to the fatal battle of Camlann at which Arthur fell.

When the *Historia* was completed, in 1136, the manuscript was copied throughout Britain and Europe, and soon others were making their own translations and adding further

Arthur in battle

embellishments. This happened so rapidly, that it is evident there was an enormous body of previously unrecorded work just waiting for an opportunity. The distinction between fact, legend and fiction rapidly became blurred and impossible to entangle. Within a single lifetime from the completion of Geoffrey's *Historia* almost a dozen other works appeared. There was the *Roman de Brut* completed in 1155 by the Norman monk Wace, from the isle of Jersey, which introduced the concept of the Round Table. The English monk Layamon adapted Wace's work as *Brut*, written in the 1190s, during the reign of Richard I. Layamon's work was the first to render the Arthurian legend into English and, unlike the more chivalric version by Wace, Layamon made Arthur a more brutal king. This dichotomy lives on in the later works where heroic deeds sit rather strangely alongside acts of unrelenting violence.

Most of the next generation of Arthurian writings come from Norman France. Whereas the Welsh/English works had been intended as histories, albeit somewhat embellished, the later stories were blatant tales of heroic adventures, often with a mystical flavour. Chrétien de Troyes, the father of the medieval romances of chivalry, began his tales with *Erec et Enide* (*c.* 1170), and went on to create *Le Chevalier de la Charrette* (*c.* 1177) which introduced Lancelot, and the unfinished *Le Conte du Graal* (*c.* 1182) which introduced Perceval and the Quest for the Holy Grail. Chrétien was followed by the monk Robert de Boron who produced his own Grail story, *Joseph d'Arimathie* (*c.* 1190), the highly influential *Merlin* (*c.* 1200), and the incomplete *Perceval*. Then there was Marie de

France, the half-sister of Henry II, who composed several 'lays' or ballads, including Chèvrefeuil (*c.* 1200), which brought the story of Tristan and Isolde into the Arthurian canon.

The Normans' intention, to make Arthur an Anglo-Norman hero, had worked only too well. Arthur, through his heroic deeds and those of his knights, became the perfect model for the Crusades, and was adopted by the Crusader Knights, especially the French. It was through this connection, and especially the works of Wace and Chrétien, that the world of chivalry and knightly derring-do developed around Arthur. Although these tales had shifted in time over six hundred years, their origin, which essentially told of a besieged king conquering his enemies and establishing a Golden Age, was equally appro-

priate to the periods of the Welsh battles
against the Normans at the start of the twelfth
century, the English Civil War in the middle
of that century, and the Crusades against the
infidel at the end of the century. By now,
though, Arthur bore no resemblance to any
historical figure. He stood as a glorified reflec-
tion of the Crusader kings, Richard I, the
Lion-Heart, of England and Philip II of
France. Richard I would have been succeeded
by a King Arthur. After his death in 1199, his
nephew Arthur, then only 12, should have
been king, but his uncle John seized the
throne and had him imprisoned and later
killed.

Over twenty more Arthurian texts appeared
during the next two centuries. There was
Parzival by the German poet Wolfram von
Eschenbach, written *c.* 1210, which com-

pleted the unfinished work by Chrétien. There was a whole series of prose manuscripts, now called the Vulgate Cycle, written around 1215–1235, which firmly enmeshed the Arthurian and Grail legends and included the first *La Mort le Roi Artu* as its climax. A century later, an anonymous poet produced what is regarded as one of the highlights of medieval English literature, *Sir Gawaine and the Green Knight*, completed around the year 1380. And then came *Le Morte d'Arthur*, the best known of them all, completed by Sir Thomas Malory around 1470. It came into the possession of William Caxton and was one of the first books to be printed in England, coming off his presses in July 1485 – a significant year in English history, marking the end of the Wars of the Roses, and the accession to the throne of Henry Tudor as Henry VII of England.

Henry had his own designs on subduing the Welsh who, at the beginning of the fifteenth century, had rebelled against English overlordship under their prince Owain Glendower. Henry was related to Glendower through his great-grandfather Maredudd ap Tudor, and the Welsh no doubt thought that in Henry they would regain their independence. Henry had no such intention but, as part of his plan, he named his first-born son Arthur. He was born in 1486, the year after the publication of *Le Morte d'Arthur*. He duly became Prince of Wales, but died in 1502, aged only 15, and once again England was denied a new King Arthur. Nevertheless, the belief that a king bearing the name of Arthur would be able to reunite the kingdoms of Britain was clearly held by both Henry II and by Henry VII, and it is ironic that both of these heirs died at such a young age. Perhaps had England had a true King Arthur his life would have eclipsed that of the legend. In fact, when Prince Arthur died, the new heir to the throne was his brother, who became Henry VIII, and he sought to do exactly that. In Henry VIII we find an Arthurian-style king, 'Defender of the Faith', establishing a kingdom that went on to rule the waves.

Henry VIII ruled exactly a thousand years after the real Arthur. Having explored the legend and the world in which it evolved, it is time to peel back the layers of time to find the real King Arthur.

THE END OF THE WORLD

The world in which we encounter Arthur was one of constant strife. For nearly four hundred years much of Britain had been part of the Roman Empire, but the Romans never conquered the whole of the British Isles; their provinces covered most of what is now called England, and extended a small way into Scotland, but never covered all of Scotland, nor most of Cumbria, Wales, Devon or Cornwall, and certainly not Ireland. For all the uneasy peace sustained in the Islands for over three hundred years, the true Celts never became Romanized. By the end of the fourth century the Empire was being harried on all fronts by the many tribes of Europe. Rome began to call troops back from Britain to help fight on other frontiers, and a weakened Britain found herself under greater attack from the Saxons. Even whilst Roman rule remained, the British began to elect their own leaders. One of these, Magnus Clemens Maximus, who had helped defend Britain against the Saxons, became so popular that he raised an army in Britain and marched on Rome. He held the city for two years as Emperor before being defeated and killed in AD 388. His triumph was treasured by the British who remembered him in folklore as Macsen, the man who conquered Rome. His glory was short-lived, but the memory of his exploits later became associated with the triumphs of Arthur.

Although Britain now lacked a leader of strength and character, Rome's hold on the land was slackening. In AD 419 a Roman expedition to Britain was organized by the Church under Pope Celestine. He sent Germanus, a former soldier and administrator but now Bishop of Auxerre, to strengthen the spirit of the British Christians against pagan pressures. Near Chester, Germanus found himself under attack by the Celts of the north. Reverting to his soldier's training, Germanus repulsed them, holding his cross high and shouting 'Alleluia!' This famous victory came to epitomize the triumph of Christianity over paganism which again became symbolic in the Arthurian legend.

In southern England, by the time of the visit of Germanus, some semblance of organization existed between the remaining Romans and

the leading British Celts. The leader of the
British Celts in the South at this time was a
man who has come to be known as Vortigern,
a name which is really a title, meaning 'overlord'. His reputation has not come well down
the years. He was a powerful nobleman, who
married the daughter of Magnus Maximus,
and sought to regain Celtic authority over
Britain. To do so he not only had to over-
come the last vestige of Roman rule, and quell
the northern Celts, but he also had to defeat
the Saxon invaders. This was no easy task, and
Vortigern made the wrong decision. He
entered into an alliance with the Jutish war-
leader, Hengist, against the northern Celts and
Romans. For this reason Vortigern is regarded
as a traitor in the Celtic histories. His ploy
backfired. After just six years, during which
time Hengist and his followers had firmly
established themselves in Kent, they turned

their might against Vortigern and defeated him in the year 455. Vortigern fled into the mountains of Wales, leaving Britain exposed to the Saxons. Over the next 40 years, wave upon wave of Saxons, Angles and Jutes came from mainland Europe to conquer and settle in lands around the British coast, especially in the south, and then to penetrate inland. We can imagine, therefore, an island under siege from Germanic invaders to the south and east and, by the end of the fifth century, from the north. The Saxons showed no mercy, plundering and laying waste to the Celtic and Roman townships.

The surviving Celts again looked for a leader amongst them. The first to appear was a Roman, Aurelian, also known as Ambrosius Aurelianus. For about fifteen years, Aurelian managed to hold authority in Britain and keep

Arthur fights the Emperor Lucius

the Saxons at bay, but Aurelian was probably an old man by now and he was not as immortal as his name implied. By about the year 475 Aurelian passes from history, and the Saxon incursions begin again.

THE AGE OF ARTHUR

It is in this period that Arthur first appears. In the terrible days after the passing of Aurelian, the British again looked for a leader. At length one emerged. Historical references to him are scant. Nennius, a ninth-century monk and historian from Bangor, calls him Arthur in his *Historia Brittonum*, referring to him as *dux bellorum*, or 'leader of battles', adding that he fought 'with the kings of the Britons', not that he was himself a king. Nennius's dates, though, are imprecise. The tenth-century

Welsh annals record in one year the 'Battle of Badon, in which Arthur carried the cross of our Lord Jesus Christ on his shoulders for three days and three nights and the Britons were victors.' The date of the battle has long remained in dispute, and has been placed variously between AD 496 and 516. Gildas, a monk at Llaniltud in South Wales, wrote a scathing attack on the weakness and immorality of the British in *De Excidio Britanniae* (*The Ruin of Britain*) in which he notes that the Battle of Badon occurred 'forty-four years and one month' prior to his writing. Gildas completed his book sometime before the year 547, so we might assume that the battle took place around the year 500.

Whether historically this was Arthur's first victory against the Saxons is not known. Nennius states that Arthur fought twelve battles against them, culminating in the glorious victory at Badon. There is probably some truth in this, as we can imagine Arthur setting out on a campaign systematically to drive back the Saxons. The locations for these twelve battles are also in dispute, with different interpretations placing them all over Britain. It is likely that they would have been in the north and east, where the new incursions were happening. The Battle of Badon has also been placed in the north – Dumbarton being the most likely suggestion.

If this is so then it raises an interesting question about Arthur. We do not know from where he came, and so have no basis upon which to assume that he emerged in southern Britain. Associations with Glastonbury, Caerleon, Cadbury Castle, Cornwall, Winchester and especially Tintagel, are all of later vintage,

Arthur duels with a Roman general

arising from years of misremembered, misunderstood and much embellished tales. That Arthur became closely associated with Welsh legend does not mean that Arthur lived in what we now call Wales. Welsh was only the Saxon word for foreigners, *wealhas*, and they applied it to all the native Britons, whether they lived in what is now Wales, Cornwall, Cumbria or Scotland.

Thus it is perfectly logical to deduce that whereas the southern Romans and British had rallied for their defence, under first Vortigern and then Aurelian, as the Saxons began to overrun the south, the northern British turned to another leader, Arthur. This would be supported by the very first reference to Arthur by name which was recorded in a poem by the British bard Aneirin who flourished a few years after Gildas. His poem, *Y*

Gododdin, celebrated the battles of the Votadini, a Celtic tribe who ruled north-east Britain, around Strathclyde, with their capital at Din Eidyn, or Edinburgh, and were in constant battle against the Saxons of Northumbria. Aneirin compares these heroes (fighting around the year 600) with Arthur, stating that they did not have the power of Arthur of old. Could it be then that Arthur was a former war hero of the Votadini, a tribe whose people later became known as the Men of the North? If so, it would explain much. Whilst the Saxons continued to harry southern Britain, their incursions into the north were certainly impeded. The *Anglo-Saxon Chronicle,* which records the victories of the Saxons and ignores their defeats, talks much about the growing strength of the Saxons in the south, but makes no mention of the north until their report that in 547 'Ida,

from whom sprang the royal race of the
Northumbrians, succeeded to the kingdom.'
This date ties in rather neatly with a later
record in the Welsh annals which, around the
year 540, records: 'The Battle of Camlann, in
which Arthur and Mordred perished. And
there was plague in Britain and Ireland.'

Later legend accords Arthur's reign as having
established a golden era of peace which ran for
40 years; this would be the period from about
AD 500–540. After Arthur's death at Camlann,
the Saxons again started to make inroads
against the Celts, so that by the year 547 Ida
was able to establish his own kingdom in
northern Britain.

Arthur, then, seems to emerge as a war leader,
who may or may not have established himself
as a king, but who maintained peace in

northern Britain in the first half of the sixth century. At this time 'northern Britain' probably extended for most of the land above a line drawn from the Severn Valley in the west to the Wash in the east, and would have continued at least up to a line from Dumbarton in the west to Edinburgh in the east. This was over half of the mainland of Britain, so it is not unreasonable to regard Arthur as King of the Britons.

Historically that is all we can deduce about him. It is frustrating that Gildas, a contemporary of Arthur, makes no reference to him by name at all, even though his death at Camlann happened within a few years of Gildas writing *De Excidio Britanniae*. Gildas could conceivably have met Arthur; he would certainly have known people who met him, and the message he was conveying about the ruin of

Britain could not have been better exemplified than by the apparent treachery of Mordred. However, if we read Gildas carefully it becomes clear that his attack is not aimed at the whole of Britain. He singles out five rulers for criticism, and these ruled kingdoms only in Wales and the south-west, the region where Gildas lived. Gildas had, apparently, been born in Dumbarton and would have known the northern kingdoms well, and probably felt tremendous allegiance to the northern kings, choosing not to compare his southern kings to them. Moreover, if Arthur was not a king but a great general, it would not have been relevant to mention him.

At the time that Gildas was writing, the north consisted of three Celtic kingdoms, distinct from the Irish/Scottish kingdoms that were being established even further north. These kingdoms were Elmet, in the area around Leeds, which was ruled by Gwallawg; Rheged, which covered Cumbria, and was ruled by Urien; and finally Strathclyde (the area of the Votadini), ruled by Rhydderch the Old. These three kings, who all ruled in the second half of the sixth century, were the natural successors to Arthur.

Urien, the most powerful, led a coalition army with Gwallawg and Rhydderch in battles against the Angles and Saxons in Northumbria and his early exploits were celebrated by the bard Taliesin in a series of heroic ballads. Sometime around the year 580, Urien was slain as a result of treachery by a rival prince, Morcant. It is easy to see how stories about his exploits would later merge with those of his predecessor, Arthur. Could it be that Urien's death by Morcant's treachery was the basis for the story of Arthur and Mordred? If so, it would explain why Gildas had not referred to it, as it did not happen in his lifetime. Urien's son, Owain, became almost as famous and his exploits were drawn into the Arthurian legend, where he is also known as Yvain.

At this time there was a local chieftain in northern Britain called Gwenddolau. At his court was another bard and prophet, Myrddin, to whom Gwenddolau turned for advice. Some of the prophecies attributed to Myrddin may have been those of St Columba, the Irish monk who had established himself amongst the Irish Scots at Iona by the year AD 570. Around the year 573 Gwenddolau was killed in the battle of Arfderydd, against Rydderch, and Myrddin went mad. This is the basis of the legend of

Merlin roaming like a demented beast in the forests of Caledonia.

The fighting between Britons and Saxons continued in the north. But there had been a hundred years, under the leadership of first Aurelian, then Arthur and finally Urien, when the British had managed to hold back the Saxon advance. In later years the events of that period, roughly between AD 475 and 575, became truncated into the life of one man, Arthur. Yet, all we know historically about Arthur is that he was a great leader, who defeated the Saxons in a strategic campaign that resulted in the overwhelming victory at Badon. This initiated a period of relative calm for the Kingdom of the North, until Arthur's defeat at Camlann. Whether Mordred was his ally or enemy at that battle is not said. After Arthur's death, Urien continued the campaigns and for a period was victorious. Perhaps there were those who at the time thought that Urien was Arthur re-born. Perhaps Arthur had not died at Camlann, but had been rescued and returned to fight again. In times of terror and strife we cling to any last hope, and that way legends are born. By the year 600 the days of Arthur had passed, and the might of the Saxons began to dominate the land. The Celts found themselves driven back into Scotland, Wales and Cornwall, and there they remembered the power of Arthur. One day, the Celts believed, they would drive out the Saxon invaders and the kingdom of Arthur would return. The seeds were sown of the legend of Arthur, the Once and Future King.